THE SHADE OF MY ANCESTRAL TREE

NASHA SOLIM

THE SHADOW OF MY ANCESTRAL TREE

NASHA SOLIM

palavro
PUBLISHING

The Shadow of My Ancestral Tree
By Nasha Solim

© Nasha Solim

ISBN: 9781912092383

First published in 2023

Published by Palavro, an imprint of
the Arkbound Foundation (Publishers)

No part of this publication may be reproduced, stored in a retrieval system, or transmitted, in any form or by any means without the prior permission of the publisher, nor be otherwise circulated in any form of binding or cover other than that in which it is published and without a similar condition being imposed on the subsequent purchaser.

Arkbound is a social enterprise that aims to promote social inclusion, community development and artistic talent. It sponsors publications by disadvantaged authors and covers issues that engage wider social concerns. Arkbound fully embraces sustainability and environmental protection. It endeavours to use material that is renewable, recyclable or sourced from sustainable forest.

Arkbound
Rogart Street Campus
4 Rogart Street
Glasgow, G40 2AA

www.arkbound.com

DEDICATION

To all the immigrant parents and my parents who sacrificed everything so their children could have something – we would be nothing without you. I love you endlessly. Thank you for all you have given and taught me. You are the real heroes.

To all the kids of immigrants who are breaking generational trauma – this one's for us.

FOREWORD

"The one who plants trees, knowing that he will never sit in their shade, has at least started to understand the meaning of life"

- Rabindranath Tagore

TEARS

A PRODUCT OF MY ENVIRONMENT

Resentment saturates and hardens
Fashioning your exterior hard
Rotting from the inside
I oozed sweetness
A peach in its prime
Turned bitter
A product of ill keeping
Self-depreciation
And malnutrition

ASIAN DAUGHTERS

Why do so many Asian girls end up with toxic men?
Because we will do anything to escape the hell that is our own homes

Our fathers taught us that a harsh word is a man's affection
Our mothers taught us that no matter how much you endure, you will never be able
To compete for their son's dedication

One finger is always wagging at you
Saying that us daughters should do better

DADA

In death you have found freedom
You had to leave me here lying
I hope that you can smell the Garden of Eden
But ironically, I am here dying

If the ego is attached to the body
Perhaps most people only really feel God in death
Ego is the kink in the evolution of man
For egoism stops us from being connected to the divine
Yet you had no aura of human desire
Some simple white cloth and tasbih beads was all you needed
You were all soul

You lived a long life
But I cannot help the feeling that you left me here lying
In your time love was rife
But now I am dying

The salt from my tears
Rubbed into the scars of my heart
I will mourn for more than years
I guess I will exchange the sorrow for art

Forever is my love
My signature bears our names linked together
We will meet at the golden gates of above
Like the green vines of our bari
We will always be interlocked

SALAAM NANA

How much pain
Can one heart take?
If God loves you then the answer is infinite amounts
I am surprised that mine has lasted so long
The hands that I have been dealt
I feel weathered away
Withered and frail
Ready to crawl into my grave

What would I not give to see my Nana
Why do I exist when you cease to?
I should have caught you when you fell
But we were selfish
The dunya makes us forget what is important
We become blinded

I miss you Nana
I was never close to you, and please forgive me for that
My heart was torn by past grievances which I should have let go of
Now my heart bleeds
I have too much pride and I am stubborn
I am young and naive
I apologise
I forgive you
I love you

But now I have been forced to let go of you
The prayer of the janaza broke through the air
Shattering my world into a thousand pieces
They lower your vessel into the ground
You lay there
But I rest knowing that 70,000 angels surround you
I entrust you with the Lord
May your grave be a garden of joy
Insha'Allah may Allah grant you the highest ranks of Jannah
I hope that you are at rest, and I can't wait until the day I get to say
Salaam Nana

Inna lillahi wa inna ilayhi raji'un
I will see you again
Salaam Nana

DAADI

My Daadi was 24 when she died
She sacrificed her life for her family
Such as the tale goes
Of the eldest daughter

Of women enslaving themselves
Torturing and tormenting their minds
Absorbing the pain of generations
Just for the sake of those they love

For too long
Women have had to risk it all
In the name of femininity
Never having their own desires but always having to endure

Without my Daadi's sacrifice
I would not be standing here
Today at 24
But with four kids to feed and even more siblings to raise

Unlike her
I have a degree and a job
Independence and my own self worth

My Daadi died of child labour
I now care for women in the holy act of birth
Today at 24 I end this curse

Daadi, thank you for all that you gave
My hands place kisses on your feet
I will always feel connected to you

You and I together
We broke this generational curse
Of women sacrificing their whole life's worth

GRIEF

Grief
My old foe
An unwelcome guest
Yet again, you have drawn up a chair

But love cannot be severed
Real love cannot be destroyed
Not everything must be tangible to exist

So really, I can never be disconnected
From those who have departed

My beloved
You are always with me
And I am always with you

For you form a part of my very being
Separation does not exist
For those who love with their soul

ANGER

Anger is the broken face of someone who just wants to be loved
Venom leaks from their mouths
When tears cannot fall from their cheeks
Fury, passion and rage
Breathing
Burning
Red hot fire
At
Desire
That is not being fulfilled

GENERATIONAL TRAUMA OF SIBLINGS

Two sides of a coin
Same heart
Ripped apart
Two pairs of real eyes
Realise
Real lies
Seeing
Horror playing out
In real time

One ferocious
One broken
Two components
Like fire and ice
We cannot exist without each other

Real recognises Real
Generational trauma bonding siblings

EMPATHS

How can I heal from trauma I am still experiencing?
Wielded as a weapon, used as a punch bag
Then tossed aside
Like I mean nothing

I am here to keep up with everyone
Hold their hand
A steppingstone
Someone to lean on
Until I almost crack

Being an empath is not something to be proud of
Always taught to put others' trauma before your own

I feel broken and weak
Used and abused
Forgotten about
Like I do not exist
A ghoul that is seen
But not heard
A fool

EMOTIONALLY UNAVAILABLE

I always seek out space in places already occupied
I have to clamour inside
Fight to survive
There is no room, there is no light
I settle for crumbs
I am starving
For anything I receive I am way too grateful
But the spaces I pour into have no capacity
They cannot retain me
So I stay forever brimming
On the edge of spaces I have occupied
Quivering
Forever in a cycle
Of constant dissatisfaction

FRIENDSHIP BREAKUPS

Friendship breakups are so painful
Because they are never direct
They accumulate in pain
Like a malignant disease
From an unknown source
A random genetic defect

You knew me better than I knew myself
As if you were part of the coding of my DNA
You helped form the building blocks
That made links and chains
Forming who I am
Intrinsically and inextricably linked
In our identity

The helix of DNA has unravelled
Our base pairs no longer aligned
The sugar phosphate backbone I once relied on
Has come undone
My genetic make up has changed

Time to learn from my mistakes
We are not a pair
But two separate entities
That forge our own sequences
Face our own consequences
Our coding meaning
We want different things in our lives
We are different beings
With changing morals and beliefs

Our expression is too different
For us to be part of the same foundation

The core of my being has shifted
I do not know how to react
But I am sticking to who I am
I do not have to adapt

LOVE AND WAR

I showed you the knives that cut me
You wielded them against me
Decked out in armour
You cower and shield away
All is fair in love and war
And neither of us shall surrender

ELEPHANT

The gun quakes in your hand
At the elephant in the room
A poacher of my heart
You torture me
But you cannot pull the trigger
A coward
So afraid
My ivory stolen
But body remaining
I can't ever forget
How the magnificent beast won't ever be tamed

SITUATIONSHIP

Breaking up with someone who was never yours
So many unspoken words
Leaving an insatiable desire
Wishing that you did more
A sadness that you do not know where to put
A guilt
For all that never was
And that could have, would have, should have
Been yours

NIGHTCLUB

A nightclub
Is all a facade
A lie
Smoke and mirrors
Drugs and alcohol
Intoxication
A release
Fleeting
Better left forgotten
We spoke the unspeakable
An escape from our real lives
Permitted to act out in whatever way

Every night in the club
We would pretend that we weren't in love
Acting out a fantasy of a relationship that would never work
Always seeking out your face in the crowd
An extra squeeze or touch permitted
We let the whole world go
And talked all night long
I could just look into your eyes
And know exactly how you felt
We said everything to each other and yet nothing at all
You were like my home
For years
We spoke everyday
How could we not be in love?

Time went by and now I finally see
How love was the greatest intoxicant of all
We were so drunk in love that we were blinded, staggering fools
However, all good shows must come to an end
But the crowd does not cheer
Standing ovation as the people gasp in astonishment
Oh the tragedy
All the love lost
But that was meant to be
Cut abrupt at the climax of the film
Alas, the Oscar goes to you
So good at pretending
Unsure of what you want
So, tell me when you push me away
Who are you running from?
Me or yourself?

WHAT COULD HAVE BEEN

If grief is unexpressed love
With nowhere to go
I wear black everyday
For I am in mourning forever
Of what could have been
A labour of love
To heave this heavy heart
That finds no home

NOT OVER YOU

Sitting on a platform in Clapton
I thought I was over you
But my heart expands against the wounds you left
About to rupture
Full of regrets

I miss you
If we must not be in each other's lives
At least let there be peace between us
Please, I've tried
My hardest to get over this
But I will be restless
Until the seas between us are calmer
A torrent torments me within
Bubbling red hot
The motion shakes me
Spilling out into my everyday

How can we go from love to total strangers
As though what we had never existed
I know you lay awake at night
Sharing the same thoughts

How fucked up is this?
But what can I do
Except pray that time will heal my scars smooth
I pray
Please God
Help me
Take this pain away

RESCUER

I was always on the side line waiting
Your biggest cheerleader
You made your claim on me
Rendered untouchable
A doll to possess and play with
I turned a blind eye
Hoping one day you would change
Frozen in a state of anticipation
Praying you would fix up
Show up
Confess your feelings
All I ever wanted
Was to stitch you up
Hold you down
Revel in real love
Holding my breath for so long rendered me
Disabled, unable
At deaths door
To save myself
I can no longer act as your saviour

HER NAME WAS HAPPINESS

I thought I would find her
Down the barrel of a gun
Or in the sweet recitation of prayer
Like honey on my lips
I drank from the well of others' tears
To subdue my own
I watered myself with their sorrow
To wash away the thoughts that cluttered my mind
A fog that would not lift
So sticky that I stuck to the most draining people
Diving into them
So I would lose myself in the process
I bruised, I cut, I crawled
Exploring every crevice of every corner
Every rough edge
Sharp turn
To find her, I searched
In books and knowledge
In status and money
In love and popularity
In babies and the old
In silence and softness
In loudness and harshness
I have ridden every wave
Examined under, over and through
I looked for her
But she was nowhere to be found
Dopamine chasing her forever

DARLING, DON'T YOU LOOK PRETTY?

Drawing black lines
To flick my eyes open
Curling my lashes to distract
Blusher – colour me a fake smile
Contour - to hide the overeating
Concealer - masks the bags under my eyes
This is my game face
You will not see my scars
This is my mask

FUCK YOU

Red hot blood
Pulses through my veins
Powering my life's decisions
High octave individuals
Loud in laughter
Adamant in anger
Sorrowful in suffering
Heart bursting in happiness
Ecstatic
Emotion clouding my life's vision
Flushing over every detail
Washing the lens with beautiful colour
Of late I feel that my tap runs cold
Maybe my ticker grew tired and old
And I became a sallow sapling
That was once a full rose
Little to say and bashful in light
There is nothing left
I have not cried in weeks
So where has all the emotion gone?
It lives in my skin
Blurs the veins
Prickles my anxiety
Shocking me very time

I am so anxious
I listened for too long to stupid people
Who told me
I was too much
Too emotional
Too soft
Too big
Too stubborn
Too loud
Not smart enough

I have had no self-worth
I have nearly ended it all
I have battled demons
I have faced death
I have been assaulted
I have been betrayed
Abused, let down and lied to by people I have loved the most
I have always put everyone else first
I grew up in a toxic home
I did not think I could be truly loved at all

I am alive for a reason
I did not die on that day
With the knife glinting at me
I threw it down
I made a heart full of quotes and stuck them on my wall
I read them until I believed in these words

I am fantastic
I am abundant
I am allowed to make mistakes
I am not reliant on anyone
I do not need to dull my emotions
To feel less
That is who I am
How I function

I am alive for a reason
So let my body do its thing
And become alive again
Only this time it's not a cycle

I remember why I'm alive
Who I am
To be a Muslim
To help others
To be brilliant
Spread my fragrance
My namesake

Stronger, faster, more resilient
I never cared what people thought about me
I was the only brown Muslim girl shouting about politics and poetry
In purple jeans
Chubby with no make up
I have never given a fuck
I am a rebel heart
And despite everything I need to remember
I am a sexy brave heart
Learning from my mistakes and injuries
I feel like me again
I am alive for a reason
This is my life
And I will paint it how I like

I have the brain of a doctor and the heart of a poet
I am two worlds colliding and for that I am brilliant
High octane individuals need to concentrate their energy
Every great has their challenges

It all went wrong
When I became afraid
It all went wrong
When I stopped shouting
Fuck you

So fuck you fuck you fuck you
World

BODY

FREE PALESTINE

This is genocide
Settler colonialism
Occupation
Eradication
Ethnic cleansing
Apartheid
Colonial powers all collude
Arming
Powering
White supremacy ideals

2 states should exist
Stolen land will never bare fruit
Soil running deep with blood

A human rights violation
Is not warranted by anyone's God
Let alone the same God

Walls occlude
Tawakkul

From the river to the sea
Palestine will be free

AFGHANISTAN

Poppy fields of crimson red flow freely as the rush of dopamine in drug addiction
Flowers planted upon mass graves
From rotting bodies flowers shall grow
Opium the blossom to grow pharma companies
So making money is eternity

Babies are born not fully formed
For how can they grow in the belly of a tortured Mother
Where soldiers lie in the mouths of thousands of raped women
Sold into slavery
Without education
You lose generation after generation
Afghan women are now lost
So where can the blame be found?

Great Britain
The USSR
America
Pakistan
Iran
China
Gulf Arab states
Have bled the land dry
A drought has occurred
Where infants play with the bones of a once rich society

Your faces have been everywhere all over this country
Yet you deny them clawing at shores
Falling off planes
Risking their lives
Thinking that the sky
Is safer than the ground below

Another country destroyed
By imperialism and greed
Like Bush looking for chemical weapons in Iraq
Accountability is nowhere to be found
Blair is a war criminal
Yet all we have learnt
Is that Western politicians
Will always claim what they desire
Money, oil and power

GUERRILLA FIGHTER - AN ODE TO BENGALI'S WHO FOUGHT FOR THE LIBERATION OF BANGLADESH

The poor are always hungry
I am starving for more
The heart of the guerrilla fighter
A protagonist
I will not stop
I will make my mark on this Earth
For my language
Blood will run

PEOPLE OF COLOUR

They don't wanna nominate us
They don't wanna save us
They don't want us in their countries
They don't want us with their men or women
Or on their TVs
They want to wipe us out
Annihilation
Elimination
Extinction
Like we don't exist

LICENSE TO KILL

The more melanin you have
The more protected the skin
So, if it is heaven sent
Why does colour give a license to kill?

I KNOW WHY THE CAGED BIRD SINGS: MASS INCARCERATION IN AMERICA

Companies profiting off of mass incarceration
Being an immigrant or of colour can put you in jail
Poor and innocent is worse than guilty and rich
Outcomes determined by wealth
Prisons designed to kill you
They want you to reoffend
Reoffenders don't have much of a chance anyway
Please let us in to
Coming through the door blasting
Wouldn't prison be better?
1 in 3 go to jail if you're black
1 in 17 go to jail if you're white
Prisons rely on the inheritance of slavery
No jobs and no right to vote
Mass incarceration wipes the civil rights movement
New forms of control made by every era
Law and order operates against people of colour
Your skin shade branding you an enemy of the state
Slavery is still here today
It just has a new name
'Criminal'

BLACK LIVES MATTER

If human beings are canvases
And I was darker
Would you paint me red?
Across the seven seas, rubber bullets pellet at knees
Millions of miles south, tear gar lingers in many a mouth
Soil caked with blood
Territory marked by loss of life
Battles for power
Are these not the same reasons that people are vocal about looting
But not about murder?
How do you think them museums got filled?
Why thousands have protested and been arrested
For four murderers to be potentially prosecuted

And white privilege is not real?
There is no more room for white guilt
Get over yourself
EVERYONE needs to help
Working 100 times as hard as your white counterparts to get to the same place
Level the playing field and see who would really win
Questioned about why destroy a community
When they gentrify majority POC areas
Ends filled with gambling, alcohol and fried chicken shops
Trap spots
Children bleaching their skin
They do not see the beauty in their melanin and within
Screaming that abortion is an abomination
Yet kicking a black pregnant woman in the belly killing her unborn child

Control must be maintained for white supremacy to continue to reign
A system cannot fail those it was NEVER designed to protect
The police uphold the interests of the white elite
The NYPD went on strike and crime decreased
Millions raised fast for Notre Dame
Yet money always comes short when it comes creating real justice
Seconds to arm a country against its own people
So they can just jam even more black men in prison

Do not think the U.K. is innocent
This country was built on the backs of the commonwealth
The Colonialism of the British empire is an atrocity
Took away the future and wiped history
Do not forget Windrush
Made south Asians the model minority
Britain's rule: Divide and conquer
It is different here you see
Racism, hatred and bigotry

It is not sufficient to be non-racist
Be anti-racist
Fight for a change
The power is in our hands
For the time is ripe for revolution
Evil can only be committed when good people do nothing

No justice, no peace
No victory, no sleep
Black. Lives. Matter.

GRENFELL TOWER

The image of Grenfell towering over Westfield
I always feel deeply ashamed
Shopping bags in hand I often contemplate
How my people died in an inferno of flames
How it could of easily been me on that estate
Rage, nothing but rage surges through my veins
Everywhere I see fire
Of course we are enraged

We sent food to brothers and sisters who were already dead
But the victims where are they?
We do not know
24 stories, 129 flats
How could you think only 72 people perished
This is a governmental cover up for mass murder.

The government are the real terrorists
The richest borough in London
Yet a sprinkler system was too expensive
But cladding cushioned the blow
The poor stuffed into a death trap
Unsafe buildings that should be waving red blood flags
Make it look prettier for the rich
So they don't feel as bad for striking the match
That set the tower ablaze
Please, I beg you explain
How there was a tax rebate
There being £274 million of usable reserves
Institutional classism and racism
Is what has occurred

Fucking bun them
Fuck the government
We have NO faith in the system
Generations of negligence of the racialised working class
Windrush brought brown and black immigrants
Decent housing and discrimination laws were not granted
Grenfell cleared the slums to enable gentrification
Hyper segregation
Splitting the nation
To create very differential qualities of life
In blocks the poor imprisoned
Over policing
Ram the cockroaches and thugs into high rise towers!
Colonisation in the British empire
Split into two
There was the same rule
The 'brightly lit' settlers town
And the village of those native 'starved of light'

Bottom line is
The poor, the forgotten, the brown, the black and the ignored
Grenfell is our monument
They want us to know
That they really don't care about us at all
If a baby can be chucked from a window
If young people were choosing to die with their families
How can I not call this a warzone?
There are still 56,000 people at risk
Of burning to a crisp
They pray everyday that they won't die

They fear for their lives
The flammable cladding waiting to be lit
And families are still not rehoused, as the Tories would hate to admit

I scream in terror
In absolute horror
These poor souls must not die in vain
This is a call to arms
Grenfell forever in our hearts
We will never forget
Justice for Grenfell until my very last breath

DESERT BOY

A desert boy
A child with nothing
Skin the colour of warm sand
His eyes as vast as the dunes around us
His hair bleached blonde by the sun
A young boy
His face so weathered that he looked three times his age
When I looked into his eyes
I saw an old soul as golden as the sand that enveloped the horizon

You see
The people who have less tend to be the most generous
He looked at me and insisted that I take a gift of a bracelet from him
He insisted and insisted it was for free despite my disapproval
He tied the bracelet around my wrist and looked into my eyes
Like he just had to give it to me
Out of pure kindness
An obligation
Ironically a child tied this evil eye around my wrist like he had to give me protection
It sounds strange but I felt like I had met this boy before
His soul seemed to know mine
And it's as if the desert stood frozen in time

You see
The people who have nothing
Are the kindest of all
The purest souls amongst this earth
They are the closest to the Lord

I know that I am a girl who lives in the West
From a place of privilege
With a roof over my head
Food and education
Money and a family
But children are children
And this world should be a space for every child to be safe

There is no child who should have to work
In order to make a living
We need to do better for our children
Protect them, guide them, nurture them
Take care of them
Love them
Children are the most precious gifts
They are the best of humanity

To the boy in the desert
You will live forever in my heart
The bracelet you tied lives on my wrist forever
I make dua for you and every child worker
That your lives forever get better
I know that we shall meet again
My brother

THANKING MY BODY

I am grateful for this body
For functioning at such high velocity and extremity
For my heart for always being kind
For my scars which are my medals of what I have survived
For my beating heart
That I am still alive

SABINA NESSA

Location on
Friends aware
'Text me when you get home'
Trainers to run
Keys grasped between my knuckles
The whites begging for mercy
I always have a busy route planned home
Eyes down
Hair tucked into my hoodie
Watch your drink
Keep your girlfriends close
Ignore them
Smile
So they leave you alone
'I have a boyfriend'
'I said no'
Catcalled from ten years old
Groping and grabbing
Incessant
Rape jokes
Slut shaming
Possessive
Obsessive
Stalking
Predators
They are all around us
They make up the world

Men - do better
Open up a conversation
Check your boys
Stand up for what is right
Act in the face of misogyny
If not all sharks
We are still terrified at any potential bite

Women have been conditioned to violence and fear
At the hands of those
Who would not be here
If a womb had not hugged them to life
Stretched and bled
Risking her life
To shed

Men
All she wanted was to walk alone

MY BODY IS A TEMPLE

I have tried to scrub you away
My breasts a sinking weight on my chest
My waist a crevice to snatch
My hand I rub raw
But I cannot seem to rid your hold on me
I visit where I was attacked
And I feel like I have arrived at my own tombstone
I guess a part of me did die that day
The part of me that was afraid
My body is not for male consumption
I am safe in myself
I have learnt that my home is where my heart lies
And that is within
I am not a victim
My body is a temple
I bow down in worship
I am not for male consumption

WHITE LIVES MATTER

Is there a direct correlation between the melanin in your skin
And the worth of your life?
Is that why
Black and brown people
Are slaughtered and denied basic human rights
Do they decide it
On a scale of dark to light?

How dare those who have made it seem
That our lives have no meaning
No worth
As if there is NO cost for spilling our blood
Taking our land
Stealing and breaking our bones
Our souls
Throwing refugees to sea
Dropping like bombs on Syria and Iraq
For no reason
A genocide of children is allowed daily
Just because they are not white skinned and blue eyed
How dare you
Diminish our human rights
Just because you are light

REFUGEES OF THE WORLD

A one-year-old baby
Orange eyed
Bundled up in dreams of the refugee
Boat swaying from shore to shore
Only hope keeping the family afloat
Fleeing from Kosovo
The captain gave the baby a chance
And so in France
A new future was born

A young man sets his eyes on England
Where he envisioned a new era
An Ottoman Empire
A business of his own
A new dawn of generational wealth begins
Painting the sunset gold

A Ukrainian man flees for Germany
Running from persecution and harm
From blue to yellow
Looking over both shoulders
Shrouded in pain
Heavy with the guilt and sorrow

A middle-aged man talks of how there was nothing left
After the fall of soviet Russia
The land barren of opportunity
No sapling could bear its head
In a land so harsh
So again the wind took him
Where a plant could grow

For you cannot blame
The fruit of the tree
When the soil is barren

A young boy gets on a train
Passport in hand
He had no bags
Just a 100 quid
The clothes on his back
The key of opportunity
Education
Was the aim of this trip and
Ever since
My father has been shopping
For a better future
And at my graduation
He made his purchase

The Ukrainian says
We are all refugees of this world
Generational trauma
Begs at our feet
So our children will not bear
The burden of crossing another land
Searching for sanctuary
Via train, boat or plane
Thirsty for a place to call our own
We are all refugees of this world

HEART

ELDEST DAUGHTER OF IMMIGRANTS

How can the closest person to you
Turn out to be
The one who hurt you the most
Who taught you that to be liked is to go along
To adhere to what others wanted
To be gentle in a world so harsh no matter the whippings
To endure as a woman
As an emotional punchbag
That to disagree is to not respect
To bend to the will of men
To adjust to succumb to their inability to express emotion
To fall for the constant guilt trip
Why must women always be the ones to pick up the pieces
Why are eldest daughters born to parent, counsel
And hold the guilt of generations
Our kindness
Innate gentleness
Taken for weakness in a world so cruel

Enough is enough
It's time to stop making ourselves smaller
Occupy all the space you deserve
We were made from sugar and spice
No more double lives
Live your truest form

MOTHER

Strength encapsulated

A warrior

Holds the home and lifts its inhabitants

Rock solid

Composed and ferocious

Pain strengthened her bones

Beautiful being

Magical touch

Mother always does know best

I came from you

I am the dream of the immigrant

I carry our dreams and with your hand

We elevate

WEB OF LIES

We took the stars out of each other's eyes
We used its light to weave an intricate web
Of this dazzling image of what we wanted from life
Our souls in this future we created in our minds
Intertwined

It looked so beautiful
I was blinded
Your stardust mystifying my dreams
I had a vision

When you said violence ahead, I saw passion past
When you said anger issues, I saw love unexpressed
When you spoke of miscalculations, I saw misguided
We just fit together so well

But I am a storyteller
A weaver of tales
Every character I justify
Empathise

What a beautiful web we created
A future of fairy tales
Folklore

Of pink poems and black guns
Of clear eyes and venomous green lies
If you see a lion bare its teeth
Do not assume it is smiling

DIVINE WOMAN

Divine woman
Strong, kind and beautiful
A fire breathing dragon
High cheek bones and sleek black hair
Evil eye shining on your neck
Armed with intelligence, pens and paintbrushes
Your heart checked with tales of misguided youth
Of childhood abuse
Classic books littered your arena
Skin care, salt lamps and boundaries
A desire for a better life
We were a match made in heaven
You taught me how to love myself
In you I saw how magical London girls are
Fierce, protective and loving
Soul sister
Lioness
Coming from nothing
You were my everything
You were the only one I trusted to look after me
We have met before
I love you endlessly
You were my rock
No one knows me like you do
Never ever will I have a sister like you
I will miss you forever
Divine woman

TWO STOPS AWAY

I grip to my seat on the tube
My fingers press down
The blood stops frozen in my hands
Heart racing, anticipation
Pure anxiety
Red ice blocks frost over my vision
Obsessive thoughts of you overtake my mind
Brain freeze
Chilling to the bone
Building my stature
Making me brittle
On the edge
I feel like I am always waiting
You're only two stops away
Folded and crumpled in my seat
Melting away
I hate to say that I still wish
For our eyes to meet again
So close yet so far away

BLUE HEART

You brandished my heart bruised
Made it beat blue
Aching and painful
This muscle lacking power
To meet the needs of my body
So I am performing substandard
Heart racing to overcompensate
A dull drumming
A slow hum
My veins run unoxidised
Rusty
Creaking and screeching
Without you

DEAR HEART

This heart was carved out for me
Created for this depth of pain
Of joy
Of hurt
An ocean in a cup
My heart overflows with love
My heart
You were made for me
And I was made for you
You beat before my brain was even formulated
For love is 50000 times more electrifying

Before and after I learnt of what logic was
You and I have been through a lot
We both know how tender and soft you are
Gentle and accepting
Proudly displayed on my sleeve
Vulnerable to be easily bruised
You have bled immensely
But with every tear and scar
The light had entered you
Illuminating me from within
The cracks permit the light to shine through
Permeating my existence
Gold, soft filters disperse through the spectrum of life
You are so pure
Shining as my most precious medallion

I am so blessed to love so deeply
For this is how us humans feel God
Every soft hearted, gentle person will be forbade from the hell fire
Perhaps because Allah knew how unkind this world would be
So soft and yet such a vitality

Why do I not protect you more?
I was so busy trying to find myself I neglected you
Forgot you
I apologise
My deepest condolences
You have done incredible things
So strong
Ripe with hearty fullness
Equipped with all I need to go on
I promise to take care of you more often
Dear heart

TWIN FLAMES

Our hearts would melt and mould to fit one another
Embrace as if they were spiritually kindred
How the halves would sigh with relief after that long squeeze
Relaxed for we were finally reunited
It was always like the last time, every time
Magnetic, electric and yet always clinging on to each other
Repelling and rotating
Obsessed but distant
But every hug got deeper and longer
As if the two souls had their own plans
And they would delve into each other no matter how far deep
I almost drowned
The two souls fought to be one
It felt like kismet
Time would stand frozen and the moments would be preserved
Sacred
If only they could last forever

Like a moth to a flame
The high if an addict
The promise of a tomorrow that would never come made the moments more precious
Breakable but real
Intoxication banished the world
Onto a plane of nothingness
Where only we existed
We were finally alone
Together
Our souls, one soul, two bodies
Ripped apart and always yearning, lingering and crawling
To my other half

LOVE OF MY LIFE

You are the love of my life
Blinded, intoxicated, enslaved
Fighting all the time, fevered with the passion of making love
We can't be friends if you always fixate on my sex
I left you breathless
Staring
Obsessed
Shouting for my attention
Circling around my affection
A Sufi's twirl in devotion
Arms around me
Eyes dewily lit
Body trembling in anxiety
Face beaming with joy
Your hand burnt with desire at the small of my back
My hands perfectly cupped your face
I showered you in adoration
Clammy hands of anticipation, at my waist
Noses almost touching
On the precipice
Cowardly
We left the cliff
The leap of faith in love too terrifying
The fall was too deep
Immense pain and darkness enshroud us
The noor of our love cannot stay alight
In another lifetime
You are the love of my life

WE WERE NOT MADE FOR EACH OTHER

We were like two broken puzzle pieces
That matched exactly
Overlapped perfectly
But just did not fit
Two broken pieces
Trying to make a whole
Forcing and breaking each other
Gaping holes
An ugly mark
Incapable of producing the bigger picture
A puzzle that cannot be solved

TIME HEALS

When a heart breaks
And you scram to quickly put it back together
Parts will be missing
In the wrong place

TILL WE MEET AGAIN

My love for you
A fixed point that has guided me thus far
The directions God has given me tell me clearly that I must leave you here
But I am certain that in the next life
Our souls will meet
So we can burn as brightly as we desire and be absent of all worries
Where we will finally reunite
And we can no longer be hindered by excuses
Where darkness will cease to exist
And we can pay for our sins
God as my witness
I loved you before this life, and surely in the next it will only deepen
At the magnitude of eternity
I do wish we met later when you weren't as bruised and confused
And I less anxious and more confident
But such is fate
I send light to you everyday
For you, I have and always will pray
I told you that I always would be there for you
And now this is the only way
Until we meet again
I love you forever

RAIN

Life now could not exist without you
I could not anchor my roots
Where the soil was barren and infertile
Incapable of nurturing my growth
Dua formed on my lips every time it rained
I prayed
Water me
I needed synergy
The mercy of Allah is shown in rainfall
Masha'Allah
For now it has rained
And it has poured
I bare witness to all the seeds in my soul
The soil fertile
It is now time to plant and grow

The downpour washed away my sins
And showed me all that I did not know
It is time for the acceptance of my dua, insha'Allah
The amount of water collected was so vast
That I nearly drowned
But I remembered that the water cycle is perfectly measured
For just the right amount of precipitation has occurred

Alhamdullilah
For now I can blossom into the unknown
Breaking into the light
Basking in golden rays
A sunflower I emerge
I realise that you were right all along

You do need rain in order to grow
Alchemist
It is time to evaporate
So form your cloud elsewhere and colour the sky grey

Please Allah, accept my dua
I do not need the rain anymore

KINTSUGI

Kintsugi
My heart broken into pieces
Golds of love
Platinums of forgiveness
Silvers of healing
Meld me back together
Scars shining precious
God is moulding me into glory
Bedazzled
I am stronger and more beautiful than ever

DAD

The burden of Fathers
Is to have watery eyes
Withered spirits
No one's hug at the end of the day
To have come here for a better life
But it is not at all what you thought it would look like

Your accent made fun of
Racism
A lack of opportunity
Ridicule and disrespect
Birthing a tendency to always look back
Yearning for a time that no longer exists
The past is where depression lives
Working 14 days in a row just to make ends meet
With kids who cannot even speak your language
Your future void of your culture
Dressed up in Nike tracksuits and hoop earrings
Frustrated
But everyone back home thinks you are living it up
The future has been taken from you
There is nothing to look forward to
Except for your children's achievements

You hold the branches of the tree over us
No matter how cold, hungry or lost you get
You hold the branches over us
To your own detriment

Dear Fathers
Thank you for all the sacrifice
Navigating of unknown waters
For tolerating disrespect
I am sorry that you are the sail in the boat
And we are the lucky passengers
You gave us the chance to change the future
For you I will make a legacy

FIRST TO GRADUATE

My graduation
I will never forget
Shabaash roaring through the great hall
My parents eyes shining with pride
Tears in their eyes
They finally saw
It was worth it all
The years of sacrifice
Early starts in Sainsbury's and late ones in petrol stations
Hustling for a house in east
So babies with a home could be born
Making money for tuition
Piano lessons and drama
Swimming
Shaping me to be someone different

My dad at 22 years old
Coming here for an education
And here I am
A master of it all

To hear my Father say thank you
It was worth it all
Even though without these immigrant parents
We would be nothing at all
They sacrificed their lives
So we could have it all

To see them beam with pride
As I walked through that hall
A party with sprinkles and a bouncy castle
Sparklers and streamers
Crowned with strange hats
I am a child at a party
Who finally got their wish
Blow out the candle
A generation's wish

A NEW ROMANCE

As birds with gilded wings soar
Sweet whisperings drip like morning dew
Fresh and awake
New directions and journeys
Deep conversations
And stomach clutching laughs
Mangos and apples swing like jewels from trees
A canopy to a river of honey
Eyes golden
Clear vision
Open hearts
The edge of certainty saturated in excitement
Who knows where we belong
I am a gypsy living where my heart desires
I know what I deserve
A sense of calm blankets over me
The top of Primrose Hill
Smoke thickening and intoxicating the air we breath
Drinking and tasting
A glorious sunset dawns
A new romance is born

A CHANCE IN LOVE

A man who actually expresses his affection
Gives his attention
Showers me in compliments
Challenges my thinking
Respects my opinion
Values my emotion
Makes me laugh
Thinks that I am smart
An equal
Why am I so scared that it will all go away
He is not your past
He is not the others
Give him a chance

DATING

Setting afire to the golden glints in my eyes
By the time my caramel eyes
Meet another scarlet sunrise
I am content in just existing
No pressure
Sunny filters and golden flecks
Sparkle through my entire vision
Sitting and sipping slowly from my own pool of honey
I am here with God's divine presence

MY BLUE DREAM

My love runs deep like the ocean
It ebbs and flows
Like the sea embraces the shore
And the ocean holds the sky
Blue wide eyes
You were like the moon controlling my tides
A full pizza pie
The horizon looked so blissful
Like silent peace
Nirvana
A blue dream whenever I closed my eyes
A perfect picture of you and I
Maybe I will always stay dreaming of you
As the ocean longs for the moon

FEEL

I have taken all the trauma to heart
Let it reside in my chest
Too afraid of impact
To let it cut through
Clean
Be free
Let the light illuminate
Through the cracks of your broken heart
And feel
For it is a beautiful thing to heal

MIND

MIND

Obsolete

Like limestone

Weathered into the ocean

Calcium stones of coasts

Jagged

My hands are cut

I tried to steer away

Oblique

The magnitude of the cave consumes me

Bleak

Heavy darkness weighs down on my shoulders

My nose drips

Will I drown?

Pressure makes diamonds

A miner of my mind

My pain is my own

Fresh, cold water rises

Submerged

Encased in obsidian

I am alone

ANXIETY

Encased in a nervous system
Where the wiring is all fucked up
Extra sparks fly
I am electrifying
But I fear that my complexity
Will be the death of me
I feel I have psycho tendencies
This is my anxiety
An overworked circuit board
Overdrive, overthinking
Foggy mind, in rusty condition
System overload
Why am I so hot?
I am afraid
But of what?

DISSOCIATION

When I was a little kid
I spent all my money on books
At night I would read and imagine
Red dragons puffing smoke
Feathered birds of paradise prancing
Silvered fish dancing
Engineering a whole new world

When I was in school
I studied to unnecessary lengths
I was terrified
Not to succeed
I knew science was not a natural fit for me
I would study, go auto-pilot
Turn off
In my A Levels I was so traumatised that I would copy passively
Escaping my own reality

When I started working
I used Instagram and Tik Tok
To put me in flight mode
At work I would zone out
Forget things
And not understand why I was so numb
So tired
For a smart girl
I would constantly make mistakes
Dissociate

For many years I have tried to turn my brain off
To avoid my thoughts
Netflix as a prescription
As a society we have become so out of touch
We must embrace our minds
Engage in conversation
Let our brains breathe
Be relieved
To overcome our battles
We must first know
What they are

It's no longer you versus me
With all your overthinking and complexity
Mind, body and soul
Let us work together
As human beings

GASLIGHTING

Sifting through the smoke
Trying to grasp fog
Beams of light I can no longer fathom
Clutching at dust
Someone shouting in the distance
A bell goes off
My ears ringing
Birds singing
My memory swinging

POST UNI DEPRESSION

Post uni depression
Feels like there is no one to talk to
Childhood bedroom feels like prison
Your own home feels like a regression
The peace you crafted for yourself now void
No longer on your own schedule
Back to being an infant
No time to yourself
Boundaries and space a demand that has to be made
Respect is expected as you return to your parents as an adult
Abiding by another's rules
Family lowkey looking and acting like strangers
You don't even know where you belong anymore
Confused
Outgrown and overgrown the environment you were raised in
Feeling bare ungrateful
You cannot believe that it is actually over
At university you live as an adult void of responsibility
And made your own family
Which has now been split up
Friends are the family you choose
And you can't even say 'I will see them all soon'
For years I did whatever I wanted with no consequence
All I had to do was have fun
Now it's getting all too real
What is the next step?
Education has given me structure my whole life
Now I am on my own
To shape my future, achieve my goals

Independent I am unsure
How to exist as an adult
Moving forward but going backwards
Back home

NHS WORKER

When your mind has been through so much
Unkindness
Obliterated with criticism and self-hate
Basking in saline
Bruised and bloodied
I have been battling for so much
I have forgotten what it means
To love
To be pleased
To be happy
When my life has no colour
Only black and white pictures
Smeared with red for danger and death
Masks to cover how we really feel
Defeated
Drained
Pale
I'm on 2%
Running somehow full speed ahead
There's so much to do
And I feel inadequate
With no fuel in the tank
I crave stillness
So I can just take a breath
To oxygenate
To run
Full steam ahead
To the future
Without corona

To the future
Where I am fully qualified
To the future
Where NHS workers are appreciated
Paid fairly and can have a break
Overworked and underpaid
We are all running on 2%

STONE

Far out

No one can reach me

Woozy

Zooming

In and out of the frame

Here but away

Lost and afraid

Vacant and gaping

Ebbing

Detached

The world spins at a million rotations per hour

Yet I am frozen in time

Numb

A sculpture to marvel at

What does it mean?

To be made of stone

PERFECTIONISM

Perfectionism carves out a mirror with a knife
Carves a smile
We can all see you bleeding
Self-harming
Stop clowning
It is nothing but destructive
Put down the knife

NO MAN'S LAND

Where do I belong
Between a cup of tea and a custard cream
Between an oily Arabian dream
And sweatshops sewing up knickers for the whole team
Between the racists and the haram police
Between the zina and the peace
Between the mosque and the reef
Between the niqabs and the bras
The treasures and the scars
The soft and the hard
Mia Khalifa and Mo Salah
Kismet, que sera sera

Beneath and in between
Like doner meat
The scraps of an empire
We are left faceless and ripe to expire
Not knowing our own identities
On the TV
All we see is bombings on our countries
I guess you can call our tribe
Suicidal and disenfranchised

DEPRESSION

Sadness comes to me every night
It circulates through my veins and trickles out through my eyes

Resting heavy in my chest
A deep darkness resides inside
Like a black hole it consumes all the light
Why can I never feel satisfied?

My sadness is uncomfortable and yet incurable
Like a wild beast that exists within me
Uncontrollable

It consumes who I am
Leaving the shell of the human that I should be
Gnawing away at my life
Rumbling and scaring people away
I feel so separate from those I love
Isolated and afraid

Sinking in my bed
Incaving me in solitude
I try to sleep it away

All my demons attack
Picking like vultures until I am bloody and bruised
I look in the mirror

A shadow with a murderously low mood

IMPOSTER SYNDROME

I am so shy
Deflated
Watered down
Easier to swallow
Less likely to cause a riot
I used to cause uproar
Be outspoken and courageous
The soul of a martyr and the spirit of a warrior
Tuned in with the key of my heart
I would die for what I believed in
Whilst singing a battle song

Imposter syndrome
A prisoner in my own body
Unable to speak
The bars are the barriers I set
Between me and what I could achieve
A cell is a safe space I guess
To feel inadequate
Unaware of how to act
I cannot properly articulate

If chickens can puff their chests aloud
Then how can an eagle not stand proud
I am not afraid to claim what is mine
My space, my time
No one is better than anyone
And this world deserves to see the real me
It took a lot to get here
So I will whistle along
I'm a fucking G!

EDUCATION

I have studied my whole life
In my room I would immerse myself in learning
Education my only hope
I was bettering myself and managing to cope

Struggling for money
Education was my ticket out of counting pennies
Free from familial pressures
The first-born daughter, first to go to university
My dad had a heart attack providing for our family
I had no choice other than to supersede
To become financially free

I have learned numerous things
Including how to love me
Who am I, what I desire
My own identity
The key to the future
No one can ever take it away from me
Education uplifted my own destiny

POWER PLAY

Made you feel powerless
Love is weakness
And I was love
You were feeble
Not in control
You chased me
Made me yours

When I told you I couldn't be close
It killed you that I was walking away
You had to push me with full force
For I was someone you could not make stay

An insecure man can never admit when he is wrong
No power play can occur
Manipulation a tool that cannot be used
You wanted what you knew you did not deserve
Someone who would not submit
Follow instructions and be complicit

We did not even work as friends
Communication an issue
I ran a mile
Yet you could only take one step
Emotionally constipated
I was your worse nightmare
I brought out things in you that you wanted to forget
I said it how it was
Held a mirror up and shoved it in your face

ROMANTIC IDEAS

Poets fall in love with ideas
Cultivated in our minds
Decorated with pretty words
Delicate tears

CLOSURE

All the closure I ever needed was in your silence
And your inaction
So don't be surprised
I said goodbye to you a long time ago

REALISM

Always looking on the bright side
Tinges your vision pink
Sunburn in my eyes
Rose tinted glasses
Hindsight is a beautiful thing

ATTRACTED TO DISASTER

The universe only reacts to what it receives
And I attracted you
Because I manifested you
You are a reflection of the mirrors of my soul
How could I not have known?
When there is a fire, I burn with desire
Excitement and attraction
To disaster

HIGH

Vibe so high
You cannot even reach my level
Raise your vibrations
I only want energy that is colossal
A peace so fulfilling
It balloons and consumes
Expansion as undeniable as the universe
So high that I have reached another planet

PRESENT

My mind is a tool
That I need not always use
Turn it off or turn it down
Or it will combust, go into overdrive
Stop working and rust
I am not my thoughts
I am a spacious intelligence
A myriad of experiences
A timeless consciousness
I am just awareness
Remaining present

SOUL

THE CHILDREN OF IMMIGRANTS

Everything I am is everything I am not
I am the motherless son with a militant father
I am the fatherless daughter with grandparents who meant love
I am the hope to be educated
I am the hope for a better life
I am the dream of the immigrant
I am the aspirations of the working class
I am the neglected middle child
I am the victim of neglect
I am ignored
I am a lack of opportunity
I am the strongest one who takes the burden of all
I sacrifice myself for my family
I am scared
I am fearless
I am kind and loving
I was built from nothing
I am a strong moral compass
I am history, books and knowledge
I am improvement and reflection
I am ferocious
I am lionheart
I am hardworking
I am thick skinned
I am community
I am the teachings of Islam
I am the meaning of strength
I am my roots

I know who I am
Forever and proud

INNER PEACE

Peace – where does she exist?
On my quest I looked
In late night endless crowds
On the countless motives I derived
In the winking sharpness of a knife
In short skirts and make up
In God and religion
In meditation and affirmation
In friends adored and lost ashore
In the boys I kissed
In love
In my books
Or my search for knowledge
Over studying
In frantic researching
In loud music
In binging TV shows

I am obsessive
I always go overboard
I toss myself into every idea and I run with it
Maybe that is why I am a bloody poet
Over loving
Over caring
Hoping to lose myself again
I engorge, submerge, submit
I've always tried to shut down my brain
So I cannot face
What I cannot retrieve from anywhere
Inner peace

UNDERDOG

I was raised to rise above expectations
A trail blazer
Flipping the tales of misfortune of generations
Never forget
My purpose on this earth is to prove you wrong
And for my entire lineage I will come out strong

UNIVERSITY

University over
I feel depleted and burned out
Unreal
Surreal
We made it
The climb
Went so fast
My sanctuary
Living with my best friends
What a beautiful life we led

I am so blessed to have loved so deeply
Lived and experienced so much
I laughed the most
I cried the most
The key to my future success
Made my parents proud
These memories my most prized possessions
University thank you for every lesson

AN ARTISTS' EXPRESSION

An artist with no craft
Is just a person in pain
A tortured soul
With no expression

GREATEST GIFT

Your absence has manifested a love for myself I didn't know
I could have
You taught me that I must put myself first
Where my mirrors mirrored your horror and pain
I see you in me
How is it that I studied you and found myself
Now I see the greatest gift you gave me
The realisation
What I deserve
Is a real love
For myself

RUIN

Now I see that ruin is a gift
The gift of transformation
God breaks your heart
Only to guide you back
To your essence
Your inner divinity
God's reflection is you
Here I am ready for endless waves of transformation

I let your loss be my ruin
So that I could transform

KNOW MY WORTH

I only spend my love on those who do not want me
Deserve me
Or know of my value
I can only spend what is in my purse
And I have been blessed with it bursting with expense
Where I'm from, it was only natural to overinvest
Collect things I did not need
Time wasting
Rendering no profit and only loss
My margins all wrong
Expenditure gone to waste
I actively chose to give to those who cannot afford me
Uninterested buyers
Who refuse to give back
Useless donations to causes that were not charity cases
But if I am so accessible to all
I am cheapened
But my time is as precious as gold
Those who cannot afford me grab me like thieves and run
My value diminished
It's no wonder why
Those who lose me realise that they cannot afford to do so
When will they ever find someone like me?
Who readily gives so much of her invaluable self in exchange for pennies
People from the dawn of time have always catted for bargains
But I cannot be treasured if those who handle me treat me like coal
It is time
To finally get to know my worth

MUHAMMED ALI

On this Earth
I was brought to be wild
Like Ali in his prime
I always come back swinging
Vocal and pretty
I was born from a family of fighters
Battling to survive
A lineage of warriors
This is survival of the fittest

The weirdo underdog
Steel in my veins
Fire in my eyes
I envision myself a fucking winner
Float like a butterfly, sting like a bee
Keep knocking them out
Keep getting back up
The world is your arena

POTATO EATERS

The garden of this world is of excess
It overflows with
Greed and expense
Materialism
Overgrown, how grotesque
Potato eaters strip back to the Earth
Bare foot in the grass, people who are purely blessed

SOUND

Words of love
Cries of pain
Sound
The waves wash over me
Vibrations transferring
Every molecule is dancing
The oscillations stretch on for eternity
Somewhere in the universe, we exist
These moments last forever

NATURE

Everything in existence is a manifestation of God's speech
So to approach a tree, a blade of grass
The ocean, the breeze
A human being, a swarm of bees
Is in worship to the Lord on your knees

ELEPHANT SANCTUARY

As I stared into this old elephant's eyes
Time stood still
As if it was just her and I
Feeding my grandmother
Who had been abused and rescued
She looked into my soul
Communicated into my spirit
I see you
An elephant never forgets
I see you and it is ok
We are rescued and safe now
I held her trunk
We have reached sanctuary

QURAN

The heart feels so much peace at the sound of the Quran
For the words of Allah are medicine to the soul
The oneness of Allah
Encoded in the hearts of all of humankind
The body relaxes as it all sounds so familiar
Like the embrace of your mother
Like coming home
It is the sound of where we were before
The Quran was made easy for remembrance
For who does not remember their birth song

FAITH

Your past is at your feet
Praying for a better future
You have a God given purpose
Serve it

This world would not be complete without your soul
God called you to this earth
And birthed you in His infinite love

The oceans, the trees, the birds and the bees
Was painted, moulded
Curated
For us all

You were made to be rewarded
Honoured, guided and adored
And with hardship, surely comes ease

Whatever is meant to be will never miss you
Even if it was beneath two mountains
And that which misses you
Was never meant for you
Even if it sits between your two lips

God is enough for us
Suffice
In Him I put all my trust

WHOLE

We are nothing but holes
For atoms are 99.9% empty space
Only Allah is self sufficient
As-Samad
Solid, impenetrable, non-hollow
So when we reach
To fill the voids in our hearts
With anything but God
We reach for nothing
We were created in pairs
Because there is only
One
Al-Ahad
The entire universe
Reflected in the soil of your spirit
Al-Wadud
The indivisible essence
Love

JANNAH

When the heart loves something
The eyes see it as paradise
Maybe this is why I have always felt lost
A refugee
Away from where I belong
Because I can never be with all those I love
This is perhaps one of the reasons why
I so deeply yearn for Jannah
Insha'Allah

GOD IS LOVE

I do not think people understand
How much Allah really loves us
He would forgive you even if your sins reached the sky
He loves you 90 times more than your own mother
If you take one step to Him
He will take tens steps towards you
Walk towards Him
He will run to you
To every cry
He will answer a hundred times
'I am here'
He is closer to you than your jugular vein
He is the heartbeat of all that lives
That is
In you and I
All around
There is love and forgiveness
Seeping through it all
Once you understand this
You will realise
That you are never alone
That fear does not live here anymore

FORGIVENESS

To forgive
Is to emancipate yourself from guilt and judgement
To be released from another's transgressions
No longer imprisoned by the expectations you held of someone else
Only trusting yourself
In ruin there surely is treasure
So forsake those who lack remorse
Or do not deserve to be forgiven
Who whisper insincere apologies
Or stay silent in defiance
They have hardened hearts
Do not let them destroy you
Holding anger and resentment within you
Circulates and fuels every foul action
Relinquishing your spirit
You deserve to have peace
Compassion and understanding
The only way to heal
Forgiveness
Freeing us from the chains of our own anger
Birthing mercy on us all

HEALING

Healing is not a linear process
At times I feel the tears free flowing, my heart broken
Other times I am full bellied, my chest proud and independent
The world is my oyster
As a woman, my being is multifaceted
I am the strongest, gentlest beast
Who ever roamed this earth
Tough as nails and as soft as ice
Terrifyingly myself, I am growing
Pain shooting through my legs, shards of glass pierce my heart
You cannot imprison me in a box
I am abundance in a world so void
Healing is trusting the process
To have faith in your Lord
To trust that it is always darkest before dawn

VOICE

FREEDOM

The caterpillar finally burst through, emerging
A blue butterfly
I am finally free
So much tension within
I did not even realise
I am truly blessed
To have kindness as my mechanism of metamorphosis
To see life through the lens of love
My brain has more space to breathe
Forgiveness has set me free
A butterfly does not miss its cocoon
It spreads its wings and lets it be

SMALL DICK ENERGY

I emancipate myself from expectation
I commit myself to self-love and healing
I love within me all the spaces that I thought were unlovable
Secret
The sweet spots
On a hiatus I reclaim myself
I am a woman
And I'm showing up for every girl who ever doubted herself
And I'm telling you
Never let a small boy make you feel worthless
Ashamed to showcase your heart
We are worthy of love
We no longer accept those who dim our lights
Who try to quench our fire
Strong women intimidate tiny males
And invigorate real men
No more small dick energy welcome my friend

TOXIC MASCULINITY

Toxic masculinity
Venomous
Why allow your poison air to breathe?
To then oxidise
So that it tastes sweet

THE FUTURE IS FEMALE

Oi
Stalking me down the road
A rabbit to a fox
I looked good enough to eat
He intimidated me
Made me very aware of my physique
I was in fight or flight
Calculating my next step
Frozen in space
Aware that this could be it
I had my last thoughts
How can I live my life like this?

So afraid
I was calm
I knew how to play him
So I tricked the fox
I luckily escaped
Ever since that day
The way he grabbed me and kissed me replays
Over and over and over again
I feel dirty and small
Weak and vulnerable
A piece of meat to be devoured
No matter my intellect
My education
My position
I will always be a woman

I am lucky to be alive
I could of easily been raped or killed
I could of been another headline
But I am here
I am alive
And it must be for a reason
I vow to live every day like it could be my last
Make my life count
Stand up for what is right
I am a feminist
I am a woman of colour
And I am not ok
I will not stop fighting
So all my sisters have safety and equal rights
We will not be the victims of patriarchy anymore
Sisters and brothers we must unite
Females we are sacred beings
Let us pave the way
The future is female

BOYS CRY TOO

Boys cry too
And there is no shame in that
There is strength in vulnerability
How my heart breaks
That many guys can't open up
Cos it's 'pussy'
When how we feel is the only treasure
We can recount in years to come

So much pressure to be 'that guy'
Who takes the time to ask
'Are you okay?'
No wonder so many are so emotionally unavailable, unable
To deal with or express their feelings
So they lash out
Angry at the world
They can never stop fronting
Decorated in cars, jewellery and designer brands
Always with their boys
Flaunting how many girls they get
All I see is insecurity, self-loathe
Fear of being seen for who they really are
Why is it so rare for guys to converse candidly
This is so harmful
Testicular cancer, suicide
The highest killer of men under 40.

CHANGE BEGINS

The ashes have burnt
The greyness crumbles
It washes away with the wind
A quiet falls
The air is still
This is where change begins

WARRIOR

People always tell me
You are so strong
One of the strongest people I know
You got this
My broad shoulders
Childbearing hips
My stomach protects my womb
I was born to fight
Born to working class immigrants
It is tradition to work hard
Familial history a lineage of pain
Struggle is within my DNA
Melanin protects me
A survivor
Let any battle commence

STRONGEST THING ON EARTH

Smile more
Why do you look like a bitch?
Well I don't owe you pretty
This is my God damn face
I need not slather it in make up or paint a smile on
So you feel like more of a man
I need not make myself thinner, smaller
To make you feel more powerful
I am not too loud
You just don't want to hear my voice
I will not be quiet
When has a man ever been told - you're too much?
My body count the hot topic
That apparently I can't be a virgin
And if I am one, then I'm somehow an angel
Well I'm no angel, I ain't saving myself
Why is the language of sex so violent?
Virginity does not even exist
I am not preserving anything for anyone
I do this for my God damn self
Yes I am a bitch
If this means I am assertive
How ironic
When the strongest thing on earth
Is a woman

WOMEN IN EDUCATION

My parents always taught me
That I must educate myself
Be independent
For education is a key
Unlocking freedom
And marriage is the last thing to think of
To educate a woman
Is to educate a generation

PAIN IS POWER

Hurt a woman
And you plant a seed
She will grow and bloom
Because women are the backbone of society
You have reminded her she does not need anyone but herself

There is power in hurting a woman
Because with pain comes growth
And to see a woman grow
Is a powerful sight indeed

WHITE FLAG

After two years
I could not even recognise your face
Screwed up in anxiety
It is like my brain forgot and I gave you the biggest smile
Then my heart sank
How much has changed
I hate to admit
But my heart still quickened
I lost my balance
I looked at you and smiled
Attempting to meet your eye
Yet again
You looked and ran away
Became quiet
Shrank in stature, skinnier
So...this is what guilt does to people
I wanted you to say something
Do something
But nothing
My mother even asked me who you were
That is how tangible the tension was
Your friends acted as if I had stabbed you
Well perhaps I forgot how much you loved me
You circled around my friend for attention
Too afraid of confrontation

It is in this moment it was cemented
I can love you for a lifetime and more
But you will never give me what I want
Because you will never change
I messaged you because I accept
That I will always love you
And that bad blood should not exist
Between those who harbour the depth of the ocean for one another
For it boils the sea
Crashing waves
Destroying and dismantling boats venturing out for a new adventure
I did it for peace
Serenity
My final wish
I surrender
I forgive
I wish you the best
It is finally the end
A love letter in a bottle
I let it go
No regrets

CONFIDENCE

When I stand up for myself
I join arms with every woman of colour
I say I deserve to be heard
Fuck a seat at the table
I deserve a throne
A chalice
A robe
A crown
Heavy is the head that bears it
And our heads have been bowed for too long
Stand, speak, scream and shout
For I am woman and my belief in myself is more than enough
There may be smarter, funnier, better looking and richer
But I am woman and my belief in myself is enough

ENERGY

Be careful of what you speak
It very may well be put into existence
Such is the law of attraction
Energy can never be destroyed, only transferred
So what you put into the world is eternal
$E = MC2$; energy and matter are interchangeable
So if DNA can be repaired through vibration and frequency
Then the vibrations of words can be postulated to affect matter
Therefore, why don't we choose the energy and sounds that surround us more consciously?
Gossip, words of negativity and toxic energy all manifest in creating you
So engage with only light, positivity and prayer
And observe how much beauty unfolds

A TALE OF TWO CITIES

Never forget where you come from
It's the root of who you are
Making you from your head to your toes
I go to work in the city
Surrounded by money and prestige
Working for the empire
Imperial and on the other side
It is the tale of two cities
Going home on the bus
Poverty surrounds me
Sadness overwhelms me
Starting salary earning more than all around me
I should be happy
But it feels so unfair
I feel so out of place
I am both but not either
No man's land
I leave the station where my father is working at 5 am
Weary eyed and weathered hands
Working away
I rush through the barriers to the other side
The rich side
Empowered my parents gave me everything so I could cross over
To give me a better life
The parents of first-generation children
The true kings and queens of this country
For them I will make generational wealth
I will make them proud
Boots in the ground

My skin is brown
Just as the poppy sprouts in my lands far away
Remembrance
I am here to stay

THE WHOLE PICTURE

Looking at it all
Sorting and organising
Shuffling and realigning
Grounding and retuning
I welcome myself back
And I say
Look at all you have done and achieved
Look at it all without squinting in scrutiny
For that's when you miss out on the whole picture
The growth has been immeasurable
I know me and only do I
So why does my opinion of myself not qualify
To be enough
For me
Looking at it all now I can say finally
I am so proud
Of the being that is I
And how insignificant the little details are
When painting the whole picture

INNER CHILD

I am forced to become
Her
The woman
I have always wanted to be
No longer a girl
I am grown
Issues of child me
Grasp me by the ankles and beg me
Look after your inner child
I hold all of my children in my womb
The fire in my belly
We all join hands
All of them kids
Are so fucking proud of you
Look up glassy eyed with tears
How far you have come and the person that you are
Gasp in disbelief
You are a warrior
It has been such a fucking journey
But better times will come
Trust the process

WHAT YOU HAVE BEEN WAITING FOR IS NOW

It comes in waves
Sometimes in tsunamis
Realisations
Epiphanies
Blinking on the horizon
Winking at possibilities
As endless as the ocean
Glinting and ebbing
It can feel all consuming
Overwhelming
Salt water cleansing the air I breathe
Inhale
Exhale
Finally
The door unlocks and twists open
Here, we arrive at the future

ACKNOWLEDGEMENTS

My dear, dear parents for all their sacrifice and encouragement. For your dedication to my education and to my quest for a better life, I would be nothing without you. You both have held my hand through all the ups and downs in life. You both pushed and believed in me before I even believed in me. I would choose you both as my parents a thousand times over. I love you both with all my heart. You are the heroes of my life and thank you for being the most loving parents anyone could ever wish for.

My brilliant brother who is half my soul. Thank you for always being there, pushing me to be better and supporting my dreams. You have always been a light for me, and I hope you know how bright you shine. There is no doubt in my mind that you will change this world for the better. There is no heart bigger and no brain sharper than yours.

My Dada for his love of reading, your love trickled down to Dad and then to me. I wish you were here to read my book. Thank you for planting the tree that shelters us and inspired the creation of this book. I can't wait to see you again.

My beautiful Sumi Aunty, your strength, selflessness and heart of gold inspires me every day. Pretty sure we are soul mates to be honest. Thank you for always listening and understanding me. You are loyal to the bone.

To my publishing family Arkbound – thank you for taking a chance on me and giving me this opportunity. You have made my dreams come true. You have enabled so many voices to be heard in my book. You are all legends, especially Riyan Hago my brilliant editor!

My friends Cara Arnold, Jawaria Hussain, Alketa Bokcui, Selina Atim, Maryam Anis, Jessica Laxaman and Ireti Adesina. This book would not be here without all of your encouragement and patience. Female friendship is everything.

My favourite teacher Mr Samuel Hiscock, you were the best English teacher that has ever been. Your lessons were truly GOATed and I will never forget them.

My young people I worked with during my time at NCS, you guys inspired me more than you will ever know. I am honoured to have known you all.

Patrick To; one of the kindest and most brilliant individuals I have ever met. You encouraged and inspired me. You gave me so much time when I really needed it. You went above and beyond and if I can be anything like you, I have really won in life.

Lastly, but most importantly, to people of colour, to women, to refugees, to immigrants, to first generation children, to the abused, the sick, the poor and the in between – this is our story. Never stop shouting.

ABOUT THE AUTHOR

Nasha Solim is a pharmacist and writer working in London. Nasha was previously a music TV journalist. She has also previously worked as a youth worker with disadvantaged youth in London. She is the child of Bengali immigrants and a first-generation Brit, born and raised in London. She is an avid traveller. Her varied experiences have inspired her debut poetry/prose collection, The Shadow of My Ancestral Tree. Writing as diverse as the Quran, A. Helwa, Rumi, Khaled Hosseini, Margaret Atwood, Elif Shafak, Rupi Kaur, Tupac, Santan Dave, Eminem, and Lauryn Hill have all inspired her work. But she believes that the biggest inspiration is life herself. Nasha is a social activist passionate about social change, politics and equity. She currently resides in her birthplace.